Illustrators
Jeffrey Anderson/B. L. Kearley
Jon Blake
Jeff Burn/Temple Art
Bryan Evans/Temple Art
Pamela Goodchild/B. L. Kearley
Donald Harley/B. L. Kearley
Hayward Art Group
Peter Morgan/John Martin & Artists
Edward Osmond/B. L. Kearley
Michael Whittlesea/Temple Art

First published in 1979 by Macdonald Educational
under the title
Peoples of the Past: The Saxons

Reprinted in 1993
by Simon & Schuster Young Books
Campus 400
Maylands Avenue
Hemel Hempstead, Herts HP2 7EZ

© Macdonald Educational Limited, 1979

Photographs
Courtesy of the Trustees of the British Museum: 39
(BL)
Courtesy of the Trustees of the British Museum/
Weidenfeld and Nicolson Archive: 45
Bodleian Library: 33(T), 43, 44(T), 54, 55(BR)
J. Allan Cash: 41
Colour Centre Slides: 17 (T, BL, BR), 39 (BR), 41
(TR), 51 (TL, TR)
Durham Cathedral Library: 44(B)
Sonia Halliday : 55(TL)
Michael Holford: 38, 39(T), 42, 48, 49, 50
Popperfoto: 11
West Stow Anglo-Saxon Village: 19

ISBN 0-7500-1471-7

A catalogue record for this book is available from the
British Library.

Printed and bound in Belgium by Proost International
Book Production

Everyday Life in
Saxon Times

Tony D. Triggs

SIMON & SCHUSTER
YOUNG BOOKS

Contents

Introduction

In the fifth century AD many of the people who lived in what are now Denmark, north Germany and northern Holland left their homes and rowed westwards. They were the Saxons. Their name probably comes from the *seax*, the short sword, that they used.

The Saxons, like their neighbours, the Angles, Jutes and Frisians, arrived in Britain as invaders. After defeating the native Britons they settled and became farmers.

The Saxon period lasted for about 600 years. For most of this time England was divided into many kingdoms. The first to become rich and powerful was the kingdom of Kent.

The next great kingdom was East Anglia. Archaeologists have found magnificent gold treasures in the royal graves at Sutton Hoo in Suffolk.

Northumbria was the third great kingdom. It was famous for its monasteries, where monks produced beautiful books by hand.

Mercia was another important kingdom. Its greatest ruler was Offa. You can still see Offa's Dyke, the huge earthworks built to keep out the Welsh tribes. The poem *Beowulf* is another reminder of Mercia's greatest days. It tells of the hero who fought many dreadful monsters.

The Saxons' real-life hero was King Alfred who ruled the kingdom of Wessex from 871 to 899. He fought the Vikings, the new invaders.

Wolves from the sea

In the third and fourth centuries AD Roman Britain was
under attack. Some of the fiercest attackers came by sea.
They landed on undefended beaches, plundered the near-
est settlement, then made a quick get away.

By the beginning of the fifth century, the city of Rome
itself was in danger. The Romans withdrew from distant
outposts like Britain, leaving the Britons to defend themselves.

The Britons' worst enemies were the Picts, who came
from Scotland. Although Saxons had also been attacking

At first Saxon warriors raided for plunder. Later they began an all-out conquest of Britain.

Britain, King Vortigern invited the Saxon chieftains Hengest and Horsa to help him defend the country. In return they received land where they could settle and farm.

Some years later, Hengest and Horsa turned on the Britons and fought them. Horsa was killed, but Hengest founded the kingdom of Kent.

There were battles for over fifty years as more and more Saxons came to Britain, determined to settle. The Britons resisted, but by about 530 most of Britain belonged to the Saxons.

Who were the Saxons?

The true Saxons came from northern Germany. However, their neighbours, the Angles, Jutes and Frisians, are also called Saxons.

Many of these Saxons lived on islands surrounded by marsh or sea. The land was poor and not good for farming. The only way to get more and better land was to take over other people's. That is why they conquered Britain.

The Saxons crossed to Britain in rowing-boats. The largest carried forty men. To reach Britain they had to row across the North Sea, which can be very stormy. Many boats must have sunk.

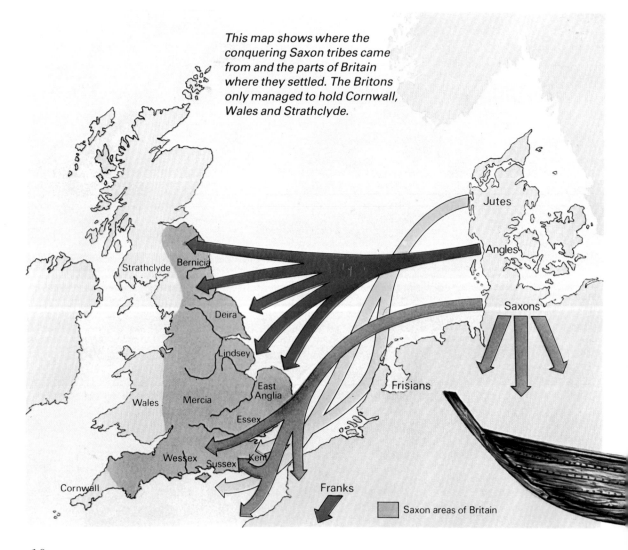

This map shows where the conquering Saxon tribes came from and the parts of Britain where they settled. The Britons only managed to hold Cornwall, Wales and Strathclyde.

Jutes

Angles

Saxons

Strathclyde

Bernicia

Deira

Lindsey

East Anglia

Frisians

Wales

Mercia

Essex

Wessex

Sussex

Kent

Cornwall

Franks

Saxon areas of Britain

◀ *Before they came to Britain many Saxons had to try to farm on very poor soil.*

▼ *Parents often passed land to their eldest son. The others had to find land for themselves.*

The invaders followed rivers deep into British territory. Their boats were narrow and easy to handle. They were also light, so the crew could carry them around obstacles.

Each boatload formed a little settlement, and the settlements grouped themselves under local leaders. At first Saxon England was a patchwork of small kingdoms, each with its own tribal chief or king. Over the years, some kingdoms conquered others, so the kingdoms became fewer but stronger. The Saxons acknowledged one king as overlord. He was called the Bretwalda.

▼ *The Saxon lands in Europe became overcrowded.*

▲ *Large areas of the Saxon homelands consisted of sand-dunes or bogs, and were no use for farming. The Frisians made artificial islands, but these quickly became overcrowded.*

▼ *The Saxons rowed their boats though they knew about sails. The boats were made from planks joined by rivets, and carried forty men. They sat in pairs, each man with an oar.*

11

Freeman and slave

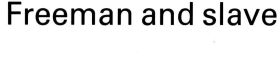

A thane and his wife. They were rich enough to have fine clothes and horses.

A churl was a freeman but he had to work hard at ploughing and other farming jobs.

Slaves, like this man, had to do the hardest and most unpleasant jobs on their masters' land.

Beneath the king, the main ranks of Saxon society were 'freeman' and 'slave'. Freemen owned land and money and many also owned slaves. If a freeman worked for another man he could leave to find another employer. The law protected freemen's rights, but also gave them duties, such as military service.

Slaves owned hardly anything. They were someone else's property. They could not leave their owner unless he sold or freed them. The law gave slaves little protection, and they were often harshly treated.

There were two ranks of freemen. The richer ones were called 'thanes' and the poorer ones 'churls'. A thane

owned at least five hides of land. (One hide was enough land to grow food for a family.)

A thane often had craftsmen, such as a blacksmith, working for him. These craftsmen were churls and seldom had any land. Instead, the thane gave them food and housing.

Other churls usually owned just one hide of land. Often very poor, they were sometimes no better off than slaves.

▲ The thane is receiving a young boy into slavery. His family are churls, and they are selling him because they are very poor. Slavery was also a punishment for crime, and prisoners of war were sometimes made to work as slaves for their captors.

The King and the law

◄ The Witan discussed new laws with the king. The Saxon word 'Witan' meant 'wise man'.

The king was the most powerful man in the kingdom. A group of the most important thanes helped him rule. This group was called the Witan.

Many Saxon laws tried to discourage vengeance killing. If someone was murdered, the victim's family felt it their duty to kill the murderer. Under the law, the murderer paid the family money instead. This payment was called *wergild*, which means man-price. The richer the victim, the higher the *wergild*. The thane's *wergild* was 1,200 shillings, but a churl's was only 200 shillings. A freeman who could not afford this was made a slave. Slaves did not have money, so they were hanged, flogged or put in the stocks and stoned.

The law was administered by 'ealdormen', who each took charge of part of the kingdom. Ealdormen had sheriffs to help them. Making sure that shop-keepers did not cheat customers was an important part of the sheriff's work.

▲ The king is receiving an oath of allegiance. The man, who may have come from a foreign country, is promising that he will be a true and loyal subject.

► The king supervised the testing of gold. A certain weight of gold was put into a water butt. If the gold was pure the water rose just to the brim but did not overflow. If the water overflowed, the king knew that a cheap metal had been mixed with the gold.

Saxon coins

If a man wounded another in a fight, a feud might start between them. This could be as serious as a feud between families after a murder. Saxon law fixed compensation for injuries, just as it did in cases of murder. A man who had his nose cut off could claim 60 shillings from the person who did it. A big toe was worth 20 shillings and a little toe 9 shillings. The payment was often made in front of witnesses. They made sure justice was done according to the law and the dispute was settled.

Jewellery for rich and poor

The Saxons clearly enjoyed wearing jewellery. Archaeologists have found many brooches, rings, buckles, necklaces and pendants. Rich people fastened their cloaks with round brooches of gold or silver. Poorer people used brooches of bronze, a cheaper material.

To make a fine gold brooch set with garnets, a Saxon jeweller first made a solid gold base-plate. Then he soldered gold wire to the base-plate to make a pattern of shallow holes. Into each hole he put a piece of gold foil and then a tiny piece of garnet.

Garnet is a dark red semi-precious stone. It is difficult to cut, yet Saxon jewellers could cut garnets down to the size of a pin-head. The gold foil had a roughened surface which reflected light. This made the stones sparkle when light shone on them.

Decorations based on animals were popular. The jewellers made the legs and bodies very long and then tangled them altogether, rather like a puzzle. Patterns like this are called animal interface.

▲ Necklaces, brooches and pins. The pins probably decorated a woman's hair. The patterned glass pendant on the necklace at the top was made by melting coloured glass rods. The other pendants are coins.

◄ Poor villagers bought jewellery from travelling pedlars.

▶ This solid gold buckle belonged to a king. It is decorated with animal interlace.

◀ This is one of the royal shoulder-clasps which were found at Sutton Hoo in Suffolk. It is made entirely of gold, except for the garnets and bluish glass which decorate the surface. The halves come apart if the central pin is removed. The two halves were sewn to the garment, which was fastened by inserting the pin.

▶ This close-up of part of a brooch shows the Saxon jeweller's fine workmanship. Some of the garnets have fallen out, revealing the gold foil which was put behind each stone to make it sparkle.

The Saxon village

Saxon buildings were made of wood, they had to be replaced when they rotted away. The walls were often made of pliable sticks called wattles. They were woven together and then covered with mud to keep out draughts. In the background is the village well.

The Saxon invaders ignored the fine towns and villas left by the Romans. They were highly skilled woodworkers and built all their houses of timber. Although none has survived, there are clues in the soil where the villages once stood. By carefully removing the top layers of soil, archaeologists can find stains left behind by rotted posts and timbers. These show the outlines of the buildings.

Saxon villages in England had groups of single-roomed buildings for sleeping, workshops and storehouses. Each group was centred round a 'hall' or meeting house, with probably one for each family.

The smaller houses were made of a framework of upright posts and horizontal beams covered with upright planks for the walls. Roofs were thatched with straw or reeds. Inside was a wooden floor with an air-space or pit underneath which could be used for storage. These single-roomed houses were five or six metres long.

The halls were much larger. They had hearths in the centre and no pits. The whole family met and lived in their hall: husband and wife, sons and daughters, uncles and aunts, brothers, sisters and slaves.

▼ *In a low hut like this one the pit gave extra headroom. Taller huts had plenty of headroom anyway, so the pit could be boarded over. A clay hearth was built on the floor. A blazing fire was needed in winter, but must have been a cause of danger. Sometimes a hut was burned to the ground.*

▶ *At West Stow in Suffolk archaeologists are reconstructing a Saxon village. Groups of smaller huts surround family 'halls'. The house with the roof coming right down to the ground is how people used to think the houses were built.*

Spring and summer

Preparing the ground for sowing with hand tools was hard work.

Each Saxon village was a farming community. Cereal crops were the most important. Wheat, barley, oats and rye were all grown. Cereals could be sown in the autumn, although spring was the main sowing season. Peas, beans and lentils were also sown in spring.

Not all crops were grown for food. Flax was grown for its fibres, which were woven into linen cloth. Woad and madder were grown for the colourful dyes they gave.

The Saxons kept cattle, sheep, pigs and poultry. They had special winter quarters, but lived in the open for the

These men are using sickles to cut the wheat. They carted it away to be threshed, winnowed and ground. Farm animals grazed on the stubble.

The Saxons cleared large areas of woodland to make new fields. They kept some woodland near their villages to provide wood for building and fencing.

These men are cutting hay with scythes. The hay was important in winter as food for the livestock. It was cut in the summer and carefully stored.

rest of the year. The pigs roamed the forests and the cattle, sheep and hens were allowed on the fields. At night they were kept in small enclosures for protection from foxes and wolves. The Saxons used dogs to herd and guard their other animals.

Poultry were kept for their eggs and meat. Cattle and sheep were kept for their milk, meat and bones. Leather was made from cattle skin. Sheeps' wool was spun and woven into cloth. Spinning and weaving were done by the women. Bones were used to make things like combs.

Autumn and winter

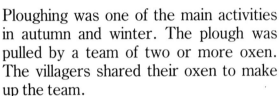

These men are burning rotten stakes. Perhaps they had been used for several years for fences, pens and enclosures.

Pruning was an important task. Dead wood was cut away so that trees and bushes grew more strongly.

Ploughing was one of the main activities in autumn and winter. The plough was pulled by a team of two or more oxen. The villagers shared their oxen to make up the team.

Each family owned separate strips of land, with a path of unploughed ground between each strip. Each year one strip in every two or three was left fallow or unploughed. Animals were kept on these strips to manure them and keep them fertile.

Most villages had permanent meadowland and woodland nearby. The woodland provided firewood and building material. In the autumn the villagers col-

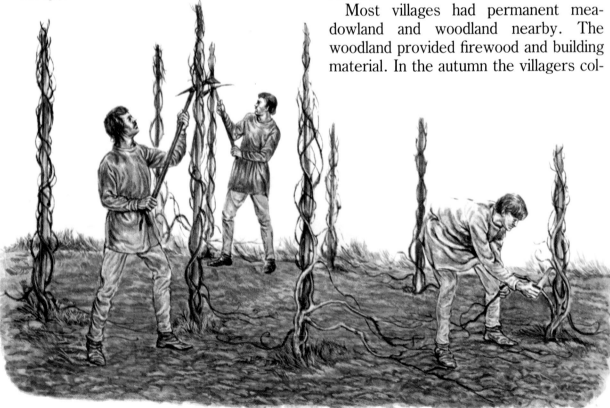

The men with flails are threshing the newly cut grain-crop to separate the grain from the straw.

lected nuts and wild berries from the woods and their pigs fed on the acorns from the oak trees.

During the autumn the villagers were busy with the grain they had harvested at the end of the summer. The grain-crop was beaten to separate the grain from the straw. Then the grain was tossed in the air. The light pieces of chaff blew away and the heavy grain fell to the ground. This was called 'winnowing'.

The dry grain was ground into flour. This was usually done with a quern made of two heavy stone discs. The top disc was turned by hand on the lower one, and the grain was ground between them.

Autumn was the season for slaughtering livestock.

A churl guides the plough. The man goading the oxen might be a slave. The other man is sowing wheat or barley.

23

Wool and weaving

The Saxons wove both wool and flax, but wool was more important. Sheep-shearing was probably done by the men. The women washed and combed the wool. Then they spun it into yarn and wove it into cloth. Besides making cloth for themselves, the Saxons also exported it.

Saxon looms were upright frames. The weighted threads of wool hanging down from the top are called the warp. Alternate warp threads were attached to a wooden bar called the heddle. The heddle had two positions. By moving it towards her, the woman pulled forward the

▼ The shepherd's job was very important. Each morning he had to drive his sheep to pasture from their night-time enclosure. He then spent the day watching over them with his dogs to protect them from wolves. He also had to repair their pens.

24

threads attached to it, so that they were in front of the others. She then passed her cross-thread (the weft) from one side to the other between the two sets of warp threads. Then she moved the heddle away from her, forcing the attached threads behind the others. Now she passed the cross-thread back in the space between them. She repeated these actions again and again, pushing the cross-thread upwards to add to the cloth she was weaving.

◄ Sheep and cattle gave a wide variety of products. Some of their milk was drunk. The rest was made into butter and cheese. They provided meat to eat and fat for using in lamps. Their bones were used for making combs, and their horns for drinking cups.

▼ The seated woman is spinning. She is turning fleece into yarn by drawing it into a thread with her fingers. She has a weighted stick called a spindle which she spins so that it twists the yarn. This gives it extra strength.

▲ Shears, loom-weights, embroidery workbox and needles. Loom-weights were rings of baked clay which were tied to the warp threads on the loom to keep them taut.

The smith and the potter

The blacksmith was an important member of the village. As well as making farm tools like hoes, spades and axes, the blacksmith also made fish-hooks, needles, cauldrons, chains and shears. He also repaired all these things. He seldom had any land.

This potter has rolled out her lump of clay like a snake, then coiled it into the form of a pot. Another method was simply to shape the mass of clay.

To complete her pot the potter has to smooth it both inside and out. This makes the thickness even and gets rid of the coiled appearance.

▲ *This man is baking pots in a kiln. He is using bellows to make the fire burn more fiercely. This means the finished pots will be reddish-brown. If there is only a little air, the pots will be black. Sometimes a potter wanted black pots and cut down the air supply deliberately.*

Saxon pottery was decorative as well as useful. Before they became Christian, the Saxons often burned their dead and put the ashes in pottery funeral urns, which they then buried. These urns were often decorated. Urns with the same design have been found in several different cemeteries. This shows there was trade between different areas.

Most Saxon potters shaped the clay by hand. When a batch of pots had dried, the potter baked them in an oven to make them hard and strong. The simplest oven was just a circular mud wall with a bonfire inside and a pile of pots in the middle. The potter kept the fire burning slowly by covering it with peat and an outer layer of earth.

Baking pots in kilns gave better results. The dome-shaped kilns were made of mud-covered wattle with a hole at the top. Before finishing the kiln, the potter stacked the pots inside. There was a hole in the base for the fire. When the pots were ready the potter let the fire go out. He opened the kiln and removed the pots. When he had another batch of pots he put them inside, repaired the kiln and lit another fire.

▼ *Larger pots and urns were decorated. Some pots have seeds baked into them. These may show what the Saxons ate.*

The fowler

Churls without much land faced starvation if the harvest was bad. To reduce this risk many churls did other work besides farming. Some worked as fowlers – they caught birds. The birds they caught were eaten by their families or sold to a rich thane.

There were different ways to catch birds: with nets, with snares, with traps and, sometimes, with hawks. The fowler made his own nets, snares and traps. He also had to catch and train his own hawks.

Each autumn the fowler lured and trapped some young hawks. He tied long strips of leather called jesses to their legs. This stopped them flying away while he trained them to bring back the birds they caught.

Then, in the spring, the fowler let his hawks go. They returned to the woods to nest and rear their young. Next autumn the fowler would catch and train some more young hawks.

The fowler always wore a strong leather gauntlet. This protected his hand from the hawk's sharp beak and claws.

The hunter

Most churls did some hunting. Catching rabbits was a good way of varying the family's meals. But there were wild boars and wolves in the woods and forests and they were dangerous. Most people took care to avoid them. Professional hunters did not. Their work depended on catching and killing the forest animals.

Professional hunters worked for the king. He gave them food and clothes in return for everything they killed. If a hunter was particularly skilful the king might give him a horse or a gold bracelet.

The usual way to catch the large animals, like deer and boar, was with nets and dogs. The hunter knew all the animals' haunts. He placed the nets he had made across the animals' tracks. Then he set his dogs to find the animals. When the dogs found the animals they chased them into the nets. There the hunter killed them.

Wild boar were particularly dangerous. Their tusks could cut through the toughest leather. They also ran very fast and, if cornered, would charge the hunter and his dogs.

Dogs, spear, dagger and net –
these were the tools of the Saxon
hunter's trade.

Games and pastimes

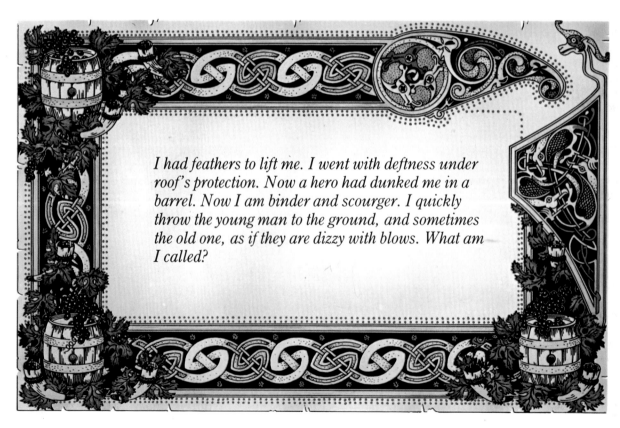

I had feathers to lift me. I went with deftness under roof's protection. Now a hero had dunked me in a barrel. Now I am binder and scourger. I quickly throw the young man to the ground, and sometimes the old one, as if they are dizzy with blows. What am I called?

▼ Villages sometimes had visits from travelling entertainers.

Heavy drinking was a favourite Saxon pastime. Feasting was popular too. At an important feast minstrels entertained the guests with music and singing. The most popular instrument was the lyre, or hand-harp, although the Saxons had other musical instruments – including the bagpipes!

At more informal feasts the lyre was passed around among the guests, with everyone taking a turn. After the meal was over there was usually dancing.

Travelling entertainers went from village to village. Jugglers and men with dancing animals were always popular.

Richer Saxons rode horses on hunting expeditions or in races. Saxon place-names confirm this. The name 'Hesketh' means 'racecourse'. There were also special sites for athletic events. These, too, are reflected in the place-names. 'Plaistow', for example, means 'games-field'.

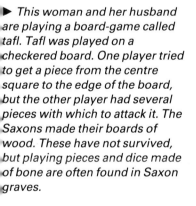

► This woman and her husband are playing a board-game called tafl. Tafl was played on a checkered board. One player tried to get a piece from the centre square to the edge of the board, but the other player had several pieces with which to attack it. The Saxons made their boards of wood. These have not survived, but playing pieces and dice made of bone are often found in Saxon graves.

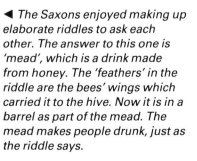

◄ The Saxons enjoyed making up elaborate riddles to ask each other. The answer to this one is 'mead', which is a drink made from honey. The 'feathers' in the riddle are the bees' wings which carried it to the hive. Now it is in a barrel as part of the mead. The mead makes people drunk, just as the riddle says.

Food and drink

Animals grew fat in the summer. They were slaughtered in the autumn and the meat was salted to preserve it for the winter.

The Saxons had to grow, catch or make everything they ate and drank. Almost nothing was imported because there was no way of keeping it fresh. Vegetables, such as potatoes, tomatoes and sweetcorn, were unknown, and so were fruits like oranges, bananas, pineapples and grapefruit.

Place-names show what the Saxons grew. It is easy to guess what was grown at Appleton, Plumstead and Peasenhall. Pears were grown at Parbold and beans at Banham. Most places, however, grew a mixture of crops, even places named after a special fruit or vegetable.

Grain crops were very important. Barley was used to brew ale and make flour for baking. Wheat was also ground to make flour. Poor people mixed different grains to make soup or gruel. They seldom ate meat. Only the rich ate meat regularly.

There is cream in the tub and the woman is beating it to make it into butter. The other woman is using wooden pats to shape the butter.

The Saxons got hardly any of their food from abroad, but ate a variety of local food. This included wild nuts and berries and game, like hares.

► *Bee-keeping was probably an occupation for experts, just as it is today.*

▼ *Pigs being kept through the winter were driven into the woods to eat acorns and beech nuts.*

Bee-keeping was important. Honey was the only sweetening the Saxons had. Mead, their favourite alcoholic drink, was made with fermented honey.

Salt was important too. To obtain it the Saxons put sea-water or salty spring water in metal pans over a fire. When all the water had boiled away, the salt was left dry in the pan. The Saxons needed salt to preserve their meat and fish for the winter. They also used it in butter and cheese.

Fish was an important part of the Saxons' diet. Archaeologists excavating Saxon villages have found the bones of many kinds of fish. The bones of pike and trout are common from inland villages, while the remains of herring, plaice and shellfish occur in seaside villages.

Meadhall and the Heroic Code

If the kingdom was in danger, the king called the freemen he ruled to stop farming and form an army. After the battle the men returned home.

The king also had a bodyguard of soldiers who lived in the royal household. In battle these men set the other soldiers a good example. They fought bravely and to the death if necessary. Even if the king was killed they went on fighting his battle. This bond between bodyguard, or retainer, and king is sometimes called the Saxons' Heroic Code.

In return for their devotion a king treated his bodyguard well. They feasted with him in his banqueting hall. The minstrel played his lyre and sang about great battles. So much mead was drunk that the halls were often called meadhalls.

The story of Lilla shows what a bodyguard might have to do for his king. A stranger arrived at King Edwin's court pretending to be a messenger. But, from the folds of his cloak, he produced not a message scroll but a dagger. As he tried to stab King Edwin, Lilla threw himself in the way. The king survived, but Lilla died.

▲ Drinking-glasses imitated the shape of the animal horns that were also used. Later the glassmakers learned that a straighter shape was better, and made fine claw-beakers (bottom left).

▶ The meadhall was a place of feasting. The warriors hung their shields around the walls. A slave served the mead and the minstrel sang songs about battles.

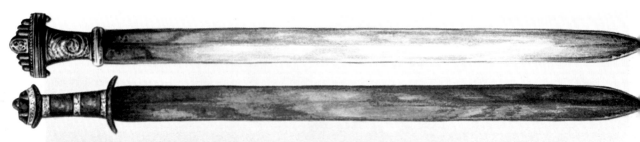

▲ Saxon kings often gave swords to their retainers. The Saxons prized fine swords. They passed them from father to son, and even gave them names.

▶ In 991, as Viking attackers overcame a Saxon force at the Battle of Maldon in Essex, a Saxon bodyguard described what loyalty meant to a retainer.

Mind shall be mightier, manhood more mettlesome,
Spirit stronger even as lifeblood streams away.
Here lies our leader, slashed by axes,
The good one cut to the ground. Let him regret it forever
Who thinks to flee from this field of battle.
Though old in years, I'll not desert
So beloved a man: I shall lay down my life
In battle beside the body of my lord.

The story of Beowulf

1 Hrothgar, king of the Danes, built a great banqueting hall called Heorot. The monster Grendel heard the noise of feasting. He found the retainers drunk and asleep. He ate thirty of them. Again and again Grendel ate Hrothgar's warriors. Beowulf heard about Grendel. He made the long journey to Heorot.

2 Beowulf kept watch in the hall while the soldiers slept. Suddenly Grendel burst in. He snatched a sleeping warrior and began to feast. Then he grabbed Beowulf. They fought fiercely. Suddenly there was a terrible howl as Beowulf tore off one of Grendel's arms. Screaming with pain Grendel escaped to die.

5 Beowulf brandished Hrunting and slashed it savagely against the monster's neck, but it glanced off. Seizing her chance, the monster came at Beowulf with a huge knife. As she advanced he grabbed a massive sword leaning against the wall. Wielding it like an axe, he cut off her head. He had saved Hrothgar's people again.

6 Beowulf returned to his home in southern Sweden. He became king and ruled in peace. Years later the peace was broken by a runaway slave who stole a jewelled drinking goblet from a burial mound. The mound was the home of a fierce dragon. Furious, the dragon flew over the kingdom spitting fire at crops and houses.

Beowulf is the Saxons' greatest poem and one of the longest poems ever written. Although written down in England in about 700, it refers to the Saxons' life in their old European homes. The hero, Beowulf, is a prince from southern Sweden. Reciting *Beowulf* was a popular entertainment at feasts.

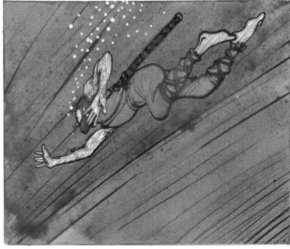

3 The next night Grendel's mother came to Heorot to avenge her son. She seized Aschere, Hrothgar's adviser, and escaped to her home in a haunted lake. At dawn Beowulf set out with a band of soldiers. They followed her tracks into lands where demons dwell. On the shore of a bloodstained lake was Aschere's head.

4 Beowulf prepared for battle. Someone lent him Hrunting, an ancient sword which had never failed. Taking it, Beowulf dived into the lake. As the murky water swallowed him up, he felt strange creatures tearing at him. Soon he was in a cave. There in front of him was the monster he was seeking, Grendel's mother.

7 King Beowulf chose a dozen comrades to go with him to kill the dragon. At its lair, Beowulf went in to fight alone. He was soon in trouble. His shield was no protection from the dragon's fiery breath. His sword could not cut its scaly skin. Most of the king's companions had crept away in fear. Only Wiglaf stayed.

8 Together, Beowulf and Wiglaf fought the dragon. The dragon sank its terrible fangs in Beowulf's neck. Blood gushed out. But, with Wiglaf's help, Beowulf killed the dragon before he died. A funeral pyre was built on a cliff top. Chieftains brought treasures, and his people built a mound over the ashes of their great king.

A king's funeral

The kings of East Anglia were buried at Sutton Hoo, near Ipswich in Suffolk. The burial site is by a river estuary. It contains several large burial mounds.

The biggest mound was opened up in 1939. Inside had been a long-ship big enough for forty oarsmen. It had been used as the coffin of King Redwald who had died in 624. The wooden ship had rotted away, but marks in the soil showed where it had been. In fact there were no signs of the king's body or his ashes. They too had dissolved away.

Archaeologists know it was the grave of a king because of the gold and jewels they found in it. These were the remains of 'grave goods', objects the Saxons believed the king would need in his next life.

▼ The hill-top cemetery of Sutton Hoo was four miles down-river from Rendlesham, where Redwald had his palace. The boat was lowered into the burial trench. Then Redwald's remains and his burial goods were put in the cabin which had been added to the boat.

◀ The Sutton Hoo helmet is made of iron, but other metals were used to decorate it. The helmet is very large. This suggests it was padded like a crash helmet. The rough, patterned pieces are what the archaeologists found.

This bird of prey is one of the decorations on the Sutton Hoo shield.

◄ The royal drinking horns were made from the horns of aurochs. These huge wild oxen are now extinct.

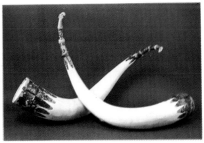

► This is the shield found at Sutton Hoo. It was made of wood and measures almost a metre from side to side. It has various metal decorations.

Saxon beliefs

The Saxons who came to Britain were pagans. They all worshipped many different gods. They made blood sacrifices to please these gods. To make the sacrifice priests killed an animal and sprinkled its blood in a holy place. The Saxons' holy places were forest clearings or wooden temples.

The town of Gateshead in north-east England gets its name from the Saxon words for 'goat's head'. There was probably a holy place there, where the head of a goat was left on a stake.

The letters of the pagan Saxons' alphabet were called 'runes'. They could be used to spell words, but few Saxons could read or write. The priests used runes as charms, and everyone understood their magical meaning.

Runes also made magic words. Some Saxon gold rings have been found with the magic word *erkiufltkriurithonglestepontol*. This was a spell to stop a wound bleeding.

The rune ↑ was used by itself as a prayer to Tiw, the god of death. Sometimes the rune ↑ was made on a sword hilt. This was a plea to Tiw to kill anyone struck by the sword.

▲ *The pagan Saxons believed that people could be pestered by elves, or by dragons and demons.*

▼ *Warriors often had boar-crests on their helmets to make them look ferocious.*

The pagan Saxons used magic spells. When they had heard of Christ they used his name or the sign of the cross in their magic. To cure a sick horse they cut crosses on its forehead, back and limbs, pierced its left ear and beat it with a stick.

▼ *Rings with runes. Runes were angular because they were often chipped into wood or stone. They were used for spells, but our modern alphabet was introduced for books.*

▼ *These urns were for human ashes. The Saxons probably believed that when the body was burned the dead person's soul was carried away in the smoke.*

The bodies of pagan Saxons were often burned to ashes when they died. The ashes were sometimes put in an urn marked with the same ↑ . This time the sign asked Tiw to receive the person whose ashes were inside.

The pagan Saxons expected life after death to be much the same as life before death. Slaves were sometimes buried with their owners, so they could go on serving them in the next life. A work-box placed in a woman's grave meant that she could continue her embroidery after death.

▲ *This picture shows a magician called Mambres. His conjuring has brought him to the brink of hell.*

▲ *Animals were sacrificed in woodland clearings like this.*

The coming of Christianity

Celtic missionaries

Roman missionaries

Aidan (635)

Iona

Columba (563)

Derry

Donegal

Yeavering (627)

Lindisfarne

Paulinus (627-634)

NORTHUMBRIA

Whitby

York

Kells

Durrow

Paulinus (625)

MERCIA

Patrick (432)

Dunwich

Dorchester (635)

London (604)

Canterbury (602)

Rochester (604)

WESSEX

Augustine comes from Rome (597)

KEY

Native British church

Extent of Celtic missionary work (634–664)

◄ *Stone crosses were erected to mark places where Christians worshipped in the open air.*

Some of the Irish monks travelled hundreds of miles, on horseback and on foot, to spread Celtic Christianity.

The pagan king of Kent and his wife listened to Augustine's preaching when he first arrived from Rome.

In 597 a group of Christian missionaries, led by Augustine, landed in Kent. They began preaching Christianity. Gradually, the pagan Saxons became Christian.

In 625 Edwin, the pagan king of Deira and Bernicia, wanted to marry the Christian Kentish princess Ethelburga. Her family refused until Edwin promised to let her bring some Christian priests with her.

Ethelburga took Bishop Paulinus with her. Paulinus worked hard to convert King Edwin to Christianity. At last he succeeded. On Easter Day 627 he baptized King Edwin in a specially built wooden church in York. As soon as he became a Christian, Edwin allowed Paulinus to preach to the rest of his subjects.

When King Oswald came to the throne in 633 Paulinus returned to Kent. Oswald was already Christian. He asked the Irish monks on the island of Iona to send him someone to replace Paulinus. They sent Aidan, who founded the monastery on Lindisfarne.

The Christianity of Aidan was Celtic. It was different from Paulinus's Roman Christianity. At first this caused problems, but the two forms united in 664.

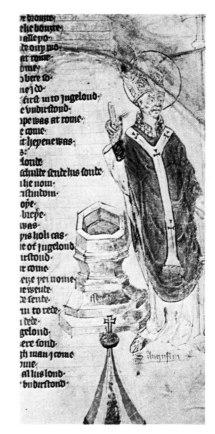

A portrait of Saint Augustine who was sent by Pope Gregory to convert the Saxons of Kent.

Both the Roman and the Irish missionaries converted many people in Northumbria. They baptized them in rivers.

Aidan travelled to Lindisfarne from Iona. The monasteries of Northumbria became centres for the spread of Celtic Christianity.

At a great meeting held at Whitby in 664, it was decided to unite Celtic and Roman Christianity into one church.

Monasteries and learning

A monk's life was extremely hard. The day began at about two in the morning, when all the monks got up to go to the monastery church for a service called matins. After that there were services every two or three hours. There was a meal in the afternoon. In winter this was the monks' only meal. In summer there was another in the evening.

Each monastery had a group of boys learning to be monks. Every afternoon they had lessons in the monastery schoolroom while the monks did farm work.

There were no schools except those at monasteries, so few people could read and write. Books were produced in the monasteries. The monks decorated the pages of the most precious books, such as the New Testament gospels, with coloured drawings and patterns.

The spread of Christianity and monasteries throughout Britain gradually led to spread of learning.

▶ *This page of the Lindisfarne Gospels says, in Latin, 'Now the birth of Jesus Christ was like this.'*

▼ *Bede was the greatest Northumbrian scholar and monk. Here he is writing a book and giving it to a bishop.*

As Christianity spread, the Saxons built churches throughout England. This one still stands at Bradford-on-Avon.

▲ *This cross, made of gold and garnets, belonged to Saint Cuthbert, Bishop of Lindisfarne until his death in 687.*

44

45

Alfred and the Vikings

In 793, Viking pirates plundered the monastery at Lindisfarne. They attacked the monastery at Jarrow in 794 and the island of Iona in 795.

These raids continued for fifty years. Then, in 851, the Vikings started to set up permanent camps on Saxon soil. They used them as military bases.

The Vikings settle

The Vikings planned to conquer England. Sometimes they made the Saxons give them money in return for staying away. The Saxons called these payments *Danegeld*. After they had got the money the Vikings usually came back to conquer the Saxons anyway.

By the beginning of 878 the Vikings had overrun all of England except Wessex, which was ruled by King Alfred. Guthrum, the Vikings' leader, planned to capture Alfred at his New Year feast, but Alfred fled. He crossed the Somerset marshes until he came to a good place for a camp. There he formed an army. When it was big enough, Alfred led it against the Vikings and defeated them.

A united Britain

The Vikings came to England as pagans, but Guthrum and his leading soldiers were baptized. They promised to leave Wessex and go back to eastern England and stay there. The parts the Vikings ruled were called the *Danelaw*.

Later kings of Wessex began to attack the *Danelaw*. Gradually they added to Wessex until Alfred's descendants ruled the whole country.

▲ *Alfred was an extremely clever child.*

▼ *In his teens Alfred fought beside his brothers.*

Alfred made his people build ships. The Vikings came to England by sea. Alfred hoped that with the new ships the Vikings would be stopped.

As king he was driven into the marshes by Viking attackers. The first Vikings were Danes, but later invasions included Norwegians.

Alfred defeated the Vikings in the summer of 878. He captured Guthrum and persuaded him to become a Christian. Guthrum and 29 of his men were baptized at Aller in Somerset.

▲ Alfred laid down new laws.

▼ Alfred married his daughter to a Mercian prince. This increased his influence in Mercia.

Alfred recaptured London and improved its fortifications. He also fortified other towns in danger of attack by the Vikings.

The Battle of Hastings

After the Battle of Hastings the Bishop of Bayeux in France ordered a tapestry to be made to tell the story from the Norman point of view. The finished tapestry is called The Bayeux Tapestry. Its pictures, embroidered in woollen thread, cover 70 metres of linen cloth!

hAROLD·REX·I

In 1042 the throne of Saxon England passed to a king called Edward. Edward was a Saxon, but had lived in the part of France called Normandy for most of his life. He had no sons, and promised Duke William of Normandy that when he died William would become King of England.

In 1064 Edward sent Harold, Earl of Wessex, on a friendly visit to Normandy. William and Harold became friends and Harold helped William put down a rebellion. William knighted Harold, who swore to be loyal to him.

However, when Edward died in 1066 Harold seized the English throne. William sailed to England to fight his former friend. Harold had just defeated Norwegian invaders in a battle in northern England, so his army was tired and weak.

When the two armies met at the Battle Hastings, King Harold was killed. The Saxon troops fled and William took the throne of England.

The Saxon legacy

The Saxons left us many things of lasting value. One was their language, which is the forerunner of several modern languages. The language spoken by Saxons who lived in England developed into modern English. The language spoken by the Saxons who stayed on the mainland of Europe gradually developed into modern German and Dutch.

In England the Saxons created the English shires or counties. Most counties and towns have names of Saxon origin. This is because many of today's towns have grown from Saxon villages.

Although the Saxons came as rough robbers and invaders, over the centuries they developed a wealthy, settled

◄ *The tower of Earl's Barton church, Northamptonshire, is a very good example of Saxon architecture. It is decorated with strips of stone. Other fine Saxon churches are at Bradford-on-Avon, Wiltshire, and at Jarrow in Northumberland.*

Saxon place-names

The Saxon word	Its meaning	Its modern form	Place-name
Burh	a fortified place	burgh, brough	**Burgh Castle** (Suffolk), **Middlesbrough**
Ceaster, Caester	a place with an old Roman fortification	chester, caster	**Manchester, Lancaster**
Ford	water crossing	ford	**Stratford, Stretford**
Ham	a homestead	ham	**Oldham, Birmingham**
Ingas	tribe or kinsfolk	ing, ings	**Reading, Hastings**
Leah	a clearing	leigh, ley	**Leigh, Burnley**
Stow	a place, often religious	stow, stowe	**Stow-on-the-Wold** (Gloucestershire), **Felixstowe**
Ton	a homestead	ton	**Bolton**

▼ This is known as the Alfred jewel. Around the edge is a Saxon inscription which means 'Alfred had me made'. It was found in 1693 near Athelney in Somerset. Perhaps Alfred lost it fleeing from the Danes in 878.

▲ This beautifully embroidered stole shows the prophet Jonah. It was put in the coffin of St Cuthbert by the Saxon king, Athelstan, in 934. Cuthbert died in 687, but people visited his shrine for centuries because he was a saint.

society. The skill of the Saxon craftsmen can still be seen in their surviving jewellery, embroidery and magnificent books. They came and built their first homes and halls in wood. Of course, none of these have survived. Later, Saxon builders became skilled stonemasons. A few of the churches built by the Saxons are still in use.

But just as the Saxons had conquered the Britons, they, in turn, were conquered by the Normans.

The story of the Saxons

AD 410

In the third century the Saxons began to attack the North Sea coasts of the Roman Empire. England was also under attack from the Picts, who came from Scotland, and the Scots, who came from Ireland.

After the Romans withdrew, in 410, the Britons were unable to defend them-

As the Roman empire declined, the Saxons began their raids on the North Sea coasts of Europe. Then they began to settle, especially in England.

selves. They allowed Saxons to settle in eastern England. In return for this the Saxons agreed to help the Britons fight the Picts and the Scots. The Saxons then turned on the Britons, and started to conquer England for themselves.

AD 597

England was already a patchwork of Saxon kingdoms. In 597 missionaries from Rome arrived in the kingdom of Kent to convert the Saxons to Christianity. They spread their work to the court of Edwin, king of Bernicia and Deira. The Irish were Christians already. They began mission-

ary work of their own in the reign of King Oswald, and many monasteries were founded. Learning flourished in the monasteries, and the monks were skilled in making beautiful books.

AD 757

Offa was one of the most powerful kings ever to rule in Saxon England. He came to the throne of Mercia in 757. In various ways, including murder, he spread his power through the whole of England, and became the Bretwalda. Proof of his power survives today in the form of Offa's Dyke, a massive rampart and ditch about 200 kilometres long. It was built on the border between the English and Welsh peoples by some of Offa's subjects living nearby. Offa's Dyke shows that the Britons of Wales were a threat to the Saxons.

Saxon villages were soon expanding. They were centres of farming, weaving and other industries. Some became towns, and continue as towns to the present day.

AD 793

In this year the Vikings began to raid North Sea coasts, just as the Saxons had done. First they came to plunder. Coasts and off-shore islands were favourite sites for Saxon monasteries. These were

Christian missionaries persuaded the Saxons to give up their pagan religion. From their monasteries they spread reading and other skills throughout England.

sacked by the Vikings. Later the Vikings began to settle. They set up bases on islands in river mouths in England, France and Germany. From these they began to overrun large areas.

AD 878

The last kingdom of England to be over-run by the Vikings was Alfred's Wessex. But Alfred made a very quick comeback. In the same year (878) he defeated the Vikings and made them withdraw to eastern England. He recaptured London in 886 and fought off a new wave of Viking attacks between 892 and 896.

AD 937

Alfred's descendants gradually recon-quered land from the Vikings and expan-ded northwards. For example, in 937 King Athelstan defeated the Vikings,

Scots and Britons in the Battle of Brunan-burgh.

AD 1016

Ethelred, nicknamed the Unready, came to the throne of England in 978. He had to fight many battles against the Vikings. In 1013 the Viking army overran a large part of England, and Ethelred fled across the Channel to Normandy. In 1016 a Viking, Canute, became king of all England.

AD 1066

With the death of Canute's son Harthaca-nute in 1042 the throne passed to Edward the Confessor, a Saxon. Since Edward had no son he promised the throne to his

The Vikings who settled half of England also settled Normandy, in France. From there these Northmen, or Normans, made a final, successful attack on England in 1066.

friend Duke William of Normandy. When Edward died in 1066 Harold was crowned instead of William, but William came and defeated Harold in the Battle of Hastings. William became King of England, so end-ing the era of the Saxons.

Famous Saxons

Alfred the Great (died 899) was king of Wessex from 871 until his death. He came to the throne at a time when the Vikings were overrunning the rest of England and even threatening Wessex itself. In 878 he defeated the Vikings and made peace with them. In 886 he made Wessex safer still by establishing a border from London to Chester. Everything to the south and west of this line the Vikings left to the Saxons. Between 892 and 896 the Vikings made further attacks, but Alfred had built strong fortifications. This time the Viking attacks failed.

As well as leading his soldiers into many battles, Alfred learned Latin. Most books were written in Latin, but Alfred wanted the best of them translated into the Saxon language. He set up a group of scholars to do this. He even did some of the work himself. He also wrote a book of laws to help his people live in peace. Alfred achieved all this in spite of a mysterious

Alfred deserved his nickname 'the Great'. He led his army, organized the building of ships and fortifications, yet still had time to write and pray.

illness which afflicted him for most of his life.

Bede (674–735) became the greatest monk and scholar of his time. When he was seven years old he joined the monastery at Wearmouth. He remained there as a novice monk for about four years.

At the age of about eleven he moved with other monks to the monastery's buildings at Jarrow, where he lived for the rest of his life. There Bede began to write the books which made him famous. The most famous, *A History of the English Church and People*, includes stories about the Saxons up to Bede's time.

Caedmon (7th century) spent most of his life as a farm worker. He was ashamed of the fact that he knew no songs. At parties every guest was expected to take a turn at singing. One day he fled from a feast in shame and hid in a cowshed. Here he had a vision in which someone stood by him and urged him to sing. Caedmon found himself singing a hymn in praise of God. He became a monk and spent the rest of his life composing religious songs.

St Cuthbert (died 687) became a monk in his teens. While still a young man he became the prior of his monastery. This made him the most important monk in the monastery after the abbot.

Cuthbert wanted to avoid an easy life, and decided to live entirely alone. With the help of other monks he built himself a hut on a rocky island. For several years he survived on what he could grow in the poor soil. In 685 King Egfrith came to the island and begged him to be the Bishop of Lindisfarne. Cuthbert agreed. He returned to his island in 687 to die.

This stained-glass window from Norwich Cathedral shows Bede. The inscription refers to his greatest book A History of the English Church and People.

out to raid Wessex. Edwin promised that if he returned successful and safe he would let a Christian priest baptize him.

Edwin's expedition went well, but he put off his baptism time and again. At last the palace priest, Paulinus, could bear it no longer. He laid his hand on Edwin's head. Edwin realized that this was the man who had pleaded with him many years before. He allowed the priest to baptize him, and Christianity quickly spread throughout his kingdom.

Edwin (died 632) was heir to the kingdom of Deira but was driven out by Athelfrith of Bernicia. During his exile a mysterious stranger came to him, begging him to stop worshipping heathen gods and turn to Christianity. The stranger laid his hand on Edwin's head. He said that this was a sign by which Edwin would know him on a future occasion. Edwin took no notice – he was more concerned with defeating King Athelfrith. In 616 he finally defeated Athelfrith and became king of Deira.

Ten years later Edwin survived an attempt on his life. The attacker had come from the king of Wessex, and Edwin set

King Edward, who reigned from 1042–1066, is known as 'Edward the Confessor'. It means he confessed, or truly believed, the Christian faith. He had Westminster Abbey built.

The world the Saxons knew

Saxon lands

Trade routes

Vikings

Missionaries

A number of Saxons made voyages of exploration. Among the explorers were Ohthere, from Norway, and Wulfstan, who was probably from Wessex. Both made reports to King Alfred.

Ohthere told of a voyage he made from his home district of Halgoland. He set out northwards and sailed along the coast for six days until he was well inside the Arctic Circle. At first he saw other ships, which belonged to whale hunters. Then for several days the seas were deserted. The land was deserted too, except for hunters, fowlers and fishermen. He then sailed eastwards for several days, and then southwards again. He saw walrus-hunting in the icy seas. He gave Alfred some tusks as a gift.

Wulfstan described how he sailed from Hedeby in Denmark to a land on the southern shores of the Baltic Sea. Here he found that the people had a strange custom when someone died. Instead of burying the body they preserved it just where it lay. Wulfstan could not explain how they did it. The body could stay in a house for as long as six months without going rotten. During this time the dead person's relatives and friends spent his money on drinking and games.

Finally the body was burned. The day began with horse-racing. The dead man's friends divided whatever remained of his property into five or six piles of different sizes. They laid them out in line within a mile of the house, then rode to a point several miles further on. From there they raced each other back. The first pile they came to was the biggest. The fastest horseman came to it first and kept the pile. The others rode on, and a little further on the second-fastest horseman collected the second-largest pile of property. When all these prizes had been collected they burned the body on a funeral pyre.

IRE LAND

CORNWAL

ATLANTIC OCEAN

SPAIN

Ohthere's voyage, about 890 AD

HALGOLAND

Origin of
East Anglian
dynasty

NORTH
SEA

OTLAND

ssionaries
5 AD

VIKING
INVASIONS
793–1066
AD

Hedeby

Wulfstan's voyage, about 890 AD

European origin of Saxons

Woollen cloth

GERMANY

Wine,
pottery,
millstones

Slave boys

FRANCE

BLACK SEA

Byzantium

Rome

First
missionaries
597 AD

ITERRANEAN

SEA

Fruit,
silk cloth,
silverware

Shells,
bronzèware,
spices

RICA

Alexandria

Foreign trade gave the Saxons
many contacts with the rest of
Europe. Slave boys were traded
across the Channel and were even
taken as far as Rome. Pope
Gregory saw some in the market
place and sent missionaries to
convert the English to
Christianity. Later, pilgrims from
England followed the same route
to Rome. Once they were
Christians the English sent
missionaries to Europe. In Saxon
times the Mediterranean became
a dangerous place for shipping.
Scarce goods still arrived from the
east, perhaps by land.

World history AD 300 to 1100

Saxons	Europe	Asia

AD 300

| Saxons were among the peoples who were attacking Britain both before and after the Roman withdrawal of 410. By 449 they had begun the all-out conquest of the native Britons. | The Huns and other barbarians were flooding into Europe from the north and east. Constant war strained Roman resources. The Emperor Constantine (306–337) ended the persecution of Christians. | The first images of Buddha were carved in China. Pilgrim[s] began to travel to China from India. Roman traders established a trading post in south Vietnam. By 400 there was a wealthy feudal society [in] Japan. |

AD 450

| By about 530 most of what we now know as England was carved up among the pagan Saxons. In 597 Christian missionaries from Rome landed in Kent. They converted Ethelbert, the king of Kent. | Rome was sacked by the Vandals in 455. Clovis, king of the Franks, became a Christian in 486. | The Huns invaded India and ended the time of peace and prosperity which Chandragupta II had established. |

AD 600

| In 627, Paulinus, one of the Roman missionaries, baptized King Edwin of Deira. Under his successor, King Oswald, an Irish monk called Aidan founded Lindisfarne Priory. The north of England soon had many monasteries. | The Moors, who were followers of the Moslem religion, were expanding into Europe by conquest. They were stopped in 732 by the Franks, led by Charles Martel. | The Tang dynasty ruled Chin[a] from 611 to 907. During that time China enjoyed a 'Golden Age' in art. Poetry, painting and porcelain reached particularly high standards. |

AD 750

| The monasteries of northern England were destroyed by the Viking raids of the late eighth century. By the ninth century the only kingdom which could withstand the Viking advance was Wessex. | In 768 Charlemagne was crowned king of the Franks. He became the Holy Roman Emperor in the year 800, and later subdued the continental Saxons. | Islamic invaders threatened northern India, but the Chola dynasty thrived in the south, and spread its cultural influence overseas. |

AD 900

| In 937 King Athelstan defeated Vikings, Scots and Britons in the Battle of Brunanburgh. However, by Ethelred's reign (978–1016) the Vikings were attacking again. In 1016 the throne of England passed to Canute, a Dane. | The Holy Roman Empire had broken up, but was later reunited under Otto I of Germany and North Italy. Brian Boru defeated the Vikings at Clontarf, Ireland in 1020. | In China the Sung dynasty (960–1279) came to power under T'ai Tsu. Though he ruled for only 13 years he ma[de] important progress in unifyin[g] the many Chinese states. |

AD 1050

| Edward the Confessor ruled from 1042–1066. He named Duke William of Normandy as his successor. When Harold took the throne William's forces defeated and killed him in the Battle of Hastings. | El Cid, the national hero of Spain, steadily pushed back the Moors (1040–1099). Pope Urban II called for the first crusade at Clermont in 1095. | The Sung administration was particularly efficient. Anyone wanting to be a civil servant had to pass three examinations. Even then only the very best graduates were chosen. |

AD 1100

Africa

Near East

America

AD 300		
…e site of Zimbabwe was …serted for hundreds of years. …e unknown 'X-group' people … Nubia buried their dead in …ch tombs. Romans closed …gan Egyptian temples in 380. …ristian fanatics wrecked …any pagan monuments.	Emperor Constantine moved the eastern capital of Rome to Byzantium, laying the foundation of the Byzantine Empire. People made pilgrimages to Jerusalem. Tombs and buildings were carved into the rock at Petra.	The Maya people in Mexico built great temples and observatories. They used their own form of hieroglyphic writing, and worked out a very accurate calendar, but they had no knowledge of the wheel, and made little use of metals.

AD 450		
…nder the Byzantine Emperor …stinian I Belisarius captured …e north of Africa in 534. It …came part of the Byzantine …mpire.	In Persia, the Sassanid Empire was approaching its height. Christians were persecuted and great Zoroastrian scriptures were written.	The Mexican city of Teotihuacan was flourishing at this time. It had more than 100,000 people.

AD 600		
…e kingdom of Ghana …overing a different area from …odern Ghana) was founded … the early eighth century. It …came wealthy from trade …ross the Sahara.	In 641 the Sassanid Empire fell to the Arabs, who imposed the Moslem religion and the Arabic language.	Towards the end of this period the Toltecs created an empire in the Valley of Mexico. The Maya civilization was also thriving in Central America. The Mayas put up calendar stones at Tikal.

AD 750		
…n the Indian Ocean coast …oslems set up trading ports. … west Africa the Hausa people …oduced fine leather goods, …d the Kanem-Bornu Empire …as founded.	An Arab, Al Razi (860–935), discovered ways of treating measles and smallpox. In mathematics, the Arabs brought the numerals 1–9 from India and introduced zero.	It has been a custom in Maya society to erect carved and inscribed stone slabs to commemorate great events. During the ninth century one centre after another ceased to erect such monuments.

AD 900		
…e kingdom of Ghana was …preme in west Africa. It …ntrolled all important trade …utes. Among the most …luable goods its traders …ndled were gold and salt.	The Byzantine Emperor Leo VI (886–912) went to war with the Bulgarians. The long campaign left the Empire's frontiers little changed, but the Bulgarians took control of the Balkans.	The Maya civilization continued to decline in Guatemala and Mexico, though in Yucatan it was different. The Maya towns in Yucatan prospered, developing their own style of architecture.

AD 1050		
…e Almoravids conquered …est Africa and coverted many … the people to the Moslem …ligion. Towards 1100 the …oruba Empire was created …ar the mouth of the River …ger.	In 1071 the Seljuks defeated the Byzantines and the emperor was forced to ask the Pope and the rulers of western Europe for help. The crusaders conquered the Holy Land but refused to hand it over to the Byzantines.	The Miztec tribe expanded under the leadership of their chief, Eight-Deer Ocelot Claw. In Peru, the Chimu people created a coastal empire, stretching for 1000 kilometres.

AD 1100

Glossary

animal interlace a design made up of interwoven animal forms.

archaeologist someone who studies the past from remains in the soil.

Bretwalda the chief Saxon king.

churl a member of the lower rank of freemen.

Danegeld money the Saxons paid the Danes to leave them alone.

embroidery designs stitched on cloth.

freeman a Saxon who was not a slave.

garnet a red semi-precious stone used in jewellery.

grave goods items buried with a dead person.

hide an amount of land.

jesses straps on the legs of a hawk.

matins a religious service.

novice someone who is learning to be a monk or a nun.

quern a pair of grindstones.

retainer a freeman who belonged to the bodyguard or household of a king.

runes the letters of the Saxons' original alphabet.

seax the Saxons' traditional sword.

thane a member of the upper rank of freemen.

thatch straw or reeds used for roofing.

warp the threads running vertically on a loom.

wattle and daub a framework of wood with clay smeared on it, used to make walls, etc.

weft the horizontal threads running across a loom.

wergild a person's money value in Saxon law.

Witan the group who advised a Saxon king.

yarn thread used in the making of cloth.

Index